From the Streets to Financial Freedom by Faith

How One Woman's Journey from Crisis to Calling Became a
Blueprint for Generational Wealth

By Dr. Angie Kelly

Dedication

This book is dedicated to the ones who were counted out. To those who survived the streets.

To those who hustled just to live.

To those who did things they're not proud of, but were trying to survive the only way they knew how.

To the incarcerated.

To the formerly incarcerated.

To the youth standing at a crossroads. If God did it for me, He can do it for you.

God never took the business out of me. Even when I was in the streets—shoplifting, pickpocketing, stealing clothes and selling them—I was still operating as a businessperson.

I was wrong. I was lost. But I was still gifted.

What changed my life wasn't that God erased who I was—He changed my partner. What the enemy meant for evil, God turned around for my good.

Today, I am debt-free and operate multiple businesses. My past didn't disqualify me—it trained me.

The
Calling Was Always There

For most of my life, I said the same thing: 'I will never work for nobody.'

For nearly forty years, I hustled. I never worked a job. Then God transformed my life, and I got my first real job at around thirty-eight years old.

Two weeks after purchasing my first home, I was fired—and that moment pushed me into purpose.

I started my first daycare, ran it for twenty years, opened another in Connecticut, and went on to build multiple streams of income.

My words weren't wrong—they were just ahead of my character. Even before my life changed, God placed a deep compassion for young people inside me.

In South Jamaica, Queens, I started a Bible study where over forty children attended. I took them to church and poured into them.

I was a foster parent for over fifteen years, choosing challenging teenagers with trauma and diagnoses—because that was my calling.

I also ministered for over twenty years inside prisons and juvenile detention centers throughout New York.

Today, I am the Senior Pastor of Second Chance Agape Worship Center and founder of Each One Reach One Radical Generation.

This is who this book is for.

Table of Contents

Introduction
From Crisis to Calling

I was raised in the heart of Brooklyn, where survival often came before dreams. My environment taught me toughness, but not truth. I fell into a life of drugs, crime, and street hustling, believing that money and power were the only way out. I made choices that led me to prison not once, but multiple times. I was searching for meaning, but instead I found madness. I lived fast, and nearly died young.

There was one night I will never forget a man pulled a gun on me. He pointed it at my head and pulled the trigger. But the gun jammed. Not once. Twice. I stood frozen as he ran off. I knew then that I was still alive for a reason. God had spared me and though I didn't know how to change, I was ready to try.

When I found Jesus, everything shifted. I got saved. I found peace for the first time. I also began to understand that God had given me talents not to hustle, but to help others rise. My journey wasn't just for me. It was to bring others out, too.

Even after God blessed me with two homes, I looked up and realized I was still in bondage this time not to the streets, but to debt. That's when my mission changed. I began to study finance through the lens of faith. I learned budgeting, credit, disputes, savings, and how to multiply income legally and biblically. Most importantly, I started teaching others.

This book is your invitation. Your road may not look like mine, but if you've ever felt stuck, ashamed, or overwhelmed by money you're in the right place. I want to walk this journey with you. Together, we're going to break cycles and build something that lasts.

Let's go. It's time to shift from the streets into financial freedom, by faith.

Lesson 1
Budgeting – Building a Blueprint

Scripture

Luke 14:28 – 'Suppose one of you wants to build a tower. Won't you first sit down and estimate the cost to see if you have enough money to complete it?'

Affirmation

I am the head and not the tail. I walk in overflow, not in lack.

Teaching & Testimony

Budgeting saved my life a second time. After the streets and the struggle, I thought owning homes would fix everything. But the truth was, I had no plan. I didn't know where my money was going. I was blessed but broke. God began to show me that being a good steward meant managing what I had. Luke 16:10 says, 'Whoever can be trusted with very little can also be trusted with much.'

A budget is not a punishment it's a plan. It's how we honor God with our finances and unlock overflow. A real budget shows you where your money is coming from, where it's going, and how to keep it working for you.

The Faith + Freedom Method

- Start by writing out your monthly income every stream.

- List all your fixed expenses first: rent, utilities, car, phone.

- Add your variable expenses: food, gas, giving, childcare.

- Assign every dollar a purpose this is called zero-based budgeting.

- Set aside a small amount each month for saving, even if it's $5.

- Review your budget every week invite God into your planning.

Use These Tools:

- Believers Budget Template

- Monthly Budget Worksheet

Faith in Action:

Print out your Believers Budget Template. Sit down with your income and bills. Say a short prayer: 'Lord, guide my hands as I plan. Help me be faithful with what You've given me.' Speak your affirmation every morning this week.

Reflection Questions

Where in your life do you feel out of financial control?

____

____

____

____

Have you been afraid to look at your budget? Why?

____

____

____

____

What would financial peace look like to you?

____

____

____

____

Lesson 2
Debt Management – Breaking the Chains

Scripture

Proverbs 22:7 – 'The rich rule over the poor, and the borrower is slave to the lender.'

Affirmation

I am breaking free from every financial chain. I owe no one anything except to love them.

Teaching & Testimony

Debt was my invisible prison. Even after I got out of jail, I was still chained not to bars, but to bills. I thought freedom meant buying whatever I wanted because I 'deserved it.' But all I did was trade physical chains for financial ones.

Proverbs tells us clearly: debt makes us slaves. And I was tired of being bound. When I started tracking my spending, I realized I was leaking hundreds of dollars on things that didn't matter. God had more for me, but I had to take responsibility first. Freedom starts with facing the truth.

It took humility to call creditors. It took discipline to say no to things I wanted in the moment. But with every bill I paid off, every phone call I made, every sacrifice I chose I felt the chains breaking. I wasn't just paying off debt. I was breaking a curse.

Debt-Free Strategy: The Snowball Method

Here's how I started and how you can too:

- List all your debts from smallest to largest (not based on interest rates based on amounts).

- Pay minimums on everything, except the smallest debt.

- Throw every extra dollar you can at that one.

- When it's gone, take what you were paying and apply it to the next debt.

- Celebrate small victories. Pray over every payoff.

You can also use the avalanche method paying off debts with the highest interest rates first but the snowball builds momentum.

Use These Tools:

- Debt Snowball Tracker

- Credit Dispute Letter (if any debts are inaccurate or outdated)

Faith in Action:

Ask the Holy Spirit to reveal any debt that needs to be dealt with first. Make a list. Print out the tracker. Fast from an unnecessary expense this week (fast food, entertainment, etc.) and apply that money to your smallest debt.

Reflection Questions

What emotion do you feel when you think about debt: shame, fear, anger, avoidance?

____

____

____

____

How has debt affected your peace and purpose?

____

____

____

____

What would life look like for you if you had zero debt?

____

____

____

Lesson 3
Credit Building – Reclaiming Your Name

Scripture

Romans 13:7-8 – 'Give to everyone what you owe them... Let no debt remain outstanding, except the continuing debt to love one another.'

Affirmation

I walk in integrity and excellence. My name is protected, and my credit reflects my commitment to stewardship.

Teaching & Testimony

There was a time I didn't even want to check my credit. I thought ignoring it would make it disappear. But the truth is, your credit is part of your reputation. It's not just about numbers it's about your name. And the Word says a good name is more valuable than riches (Proverbs 22:1).

I had to face my report. I pulled it, line by line.

I saw things I didn't recognize and debts that weren't mine. But instead of staying silent, I fought back with prayer and paperwork. I learned how to dispute, how to document, and how to rebuild. It wasn't fast, but it was worth it.

Rebuilding your credit is a faith journey too. It requires discipline, truth, and intentionality. You don't just protect your name you prepare your future.

The Stewardship Strategy

Here's how I turned it around and how you can too:

- Go to AnnualCreditReport.com and download your report

(it's free from all 3 bureaus).

- Highlight all incorrect, outdated, or duplicate items.

- Use the Credit Dispute Letter Template to challenge inaccurate info.

- Pay off small balances to improve your credit utilization rate.

-

- Open a secured credit card (if needed) and use it wisely to build a positive history.

- Keep credit inquiries to a minimum and avoid co-signing.

Use These Tools:

- Credit Dispute Letter Template

- Credit Report Checklist

Faith in Action:

Read Proverbs 22:1. Say out loud: 'God, I thank You for restoring my name and giving me favor with creditors, lenders, and future partners.' Download your credit report today and highlight 3 items to address this month.

Reflection Questions

Have you ever been taught how credit works?

____

____

____

____

How does your credit impact the dreams God gave you?

____

____

____

What would it feel like to have a credit score that reflects your growth and faith?

____

____

____

____

Lesson 4
Savings & Emergency Fund – Preparing with Wisdom

Scripture

Proverbs 21:20 – 'The wise store up choice food and olive oil, but fools gulp theirs down.'

Affirmation

I am a wise steward. I prepare for the unexpected and honor God by managing my increase.

Teaching & Testimony

For years, I lived paycheck to paycheck. Sometimes, I didn't even make it to the next one. I was always reacting, never prepared. When an emergency came a car problem, a hospital bill, or a kid needing something unexpected I would panic. And guess what? Panic leads to poor decisions: payday loans, credit cards, borrowing from the wrong people.

God began to show me that preparation is not fear it's wisdom. Proverbs says the wise store up. They don't consume everything. I started small: $5 here, $10 there. At first, it felt like nothing. But over time, I realized I was building peace. I didn't have to borrow. I didn't have to panic. I had a cushion and more importantly, I had control.

Saving money doesn't mean you don't trust God. It means you're working *with* Him, stewarding what He gives you. Faith and planning go hand in hand.

The Emergency Fund Plan

- Step 1: Set a starter goal $500 (then

- $1,000).

- Step 2: Open a separate savings account you don't touch.

- Step 3: Add a small amount weekly or biweekly even $10 counts.

- Step 4: Build toward 3–6 months of essential expenses.

- Step 5: Replenish your savings any time you use it.

Don't wait for extra money to start saving save from what you have now.

Use These Tools:

- Emergency Fund Planner

- Monthly Savings Tracker

Faith in Action:

Pray: 'Lord, help me break the cycle of panic spending. Teach me to prepare with wisdom.' Choose an amount and commit to saving it this week. Track your progress and celebrate discipline, not just dollars.

Reflection Questions

What emergency caught you off guard in the past?

____

____

____

____

How would it have been different with an emergency fund?

____

____

____

____

What are your money habits saying about your mindset wisdom or impulse?

____

____

____

____

Lesson 5
Income Streams – Unlocking Provision

Scripture

Ecclesiastes 11:2 – 'Invest in seven ventures, yes, in eight; you do not know what disaster may come upon the land.'

Affirmation

God is opening doors of opportunity. I walk in provision and purpose.

Teaching & Testimony

There was a time when I relied on just one check and when that check stopped, everything crashed. I knew how to hustle, but I didn't know how to build income that honored God and created stability. I had to shift my mindset from getting quick money to building lasting money. God showed me that provision isn't about struggle it's about strategy.

I started selling products, offering classes, and using my story to create income. I wrote eBooks, started financial coaching, and taught youth how to launch their dreams. Suddenly, I had more than one stream I had momentum. You don't need to have it all figured out. You just need to start. God will bless what you put your hands to.

The Multiplication Strategy

- List every gift, skill, hobby, or talent you have (yes, even cooking, organizing, creating, talking, mentoring!).

- Brainstorm how each one could bring income (products, services, classes, partnerships).

- Pick ONE to focus on this month.

- Create a simple action plan: what, who, when, how much.

- Pray and commit it to God. Ask for divine favor, clarity, and courage.

Don't despise small beginnings the first sale builds the foundation for the next.

Use These Tools:

- Income Streams Brainstorm Sheet

- Business Planning Template (optional)

Faith in Action:

Read Deuteronomy 8:18 – 'But remember the Lord your God, for it is He who gives you the ability to produce wealth.' Circle the income idea that makes you feel the most alive. Write out a 3-step action plan and begin praying over it daily.

Reflection Questions

What have you been sitting on that could bless others?

____

____

____

____

What lie have you believed about wealth or success?

____

____

____

____

How can you honor God with your gifts starting this week?

____

____

____

____

Lesson 6
Generational Wealth – Building a Legacy

Scripture

Proverbs 13:22 – 'A good person leaves an inheritance for their children's children, but a sinner's wealth is stored up for the righteous.'

Affirmation

I am a legacy builder. I leave a financial and spiritual inheritance for generations to come.

Teaching & Testimony

When I was younger, no one talked to me about wealth. The only thing I knew how to pass down was pain. Trauma. Debt. Survival. But God showed me that I was born to break cycles not repeat them.

Generational wealth isn't just about money. It's about mindset. It's about passing down wisdom, vision, and strategy. It's about teaching your children how to build not just pray for breakthrough, but plan for it.

I started thinking beyond my own bills. I started asking: What will my grandchildren know about me? Will they inherit a burden, or a blessing? Will they start from scratch, or will they have a foundation?

So I made a decision: I would build a legacy. I created life insurance plans. I built a will. I opened savings for my family. I documented our family vision. I wrote a book. Because my story wasn't just for me. It was for them and for yours too.

The Legacy Blueprint

- Step 1: Identify your WHY what do you want to leave behind?

- Step 2: Start a savings account or trust in your child or family's name.

- Step 3: Consider life insurance term life is affordable and powerful.

- Step 4: Create a simple will (you can revise later with a lawyer).

- Step 5: Teach your family what you learn bring them into your financial walk.

- Step 6: Document your family values and goals with a vision statement.

Use These Tools:

- Generational Wealth Legacy Map

- Family Vision Planner

Faith in Action:

Ask God: 'What is the legacy You want me to build?' Write down the names of those you're called to bless. Make one decision this week that your future grandchildren will thank you for.

Reflection Questions

What was passed down to you financially, emotionally, or spiritually?

____

____

____

____

What do you want to pass down to your children or community?

____

____

____

____

What system can you put in place this month to begin building that legacy?

____

____

____

____

Lesson 7
Faith & Finances Mindset Shift

Scripture: Romans 12:2

'Do not conform to the pattern of this world, but be transformed by the renewing of your mind.'

Affirmation: I am transformed by faith. I think like a lender, not a borrower. I walk in abundance, not anxiety.

Core Teaching Points

- Financial breakthrough starts in the mind and spirit.

- God's promises are for you, but you must believe them and act accordingly.

- Speak life over your finances daily with biblical affirmations.

- Eliminate the poverty mindset and replace it with purpose-driven faith.

Use These Templates

- Financial Affirmations List

- Devotional Reflection Page (for journaling thoughts and scriptures)

Reflection/Journal Prompt

What belief or fear around money have you carried that's not from God?

Replace it with a scripture and write out a declaration of faith.

Discussion Questions

What mindset has been blocking your financial breakthrough?

____

____

____

____

How can you renew your thoughts around money?

____

____

____

____

What does God say about wealth, stewardship, and obedien?

____

____

____

____

Bonus Lesson 8
Breaking Financial Curses – Healing the Root

Scripture

Galatians 3:13 – 'Christ redeemed us from the curse of the law by becoming a curse for us...'

Affirmation

The curse is broken. I am not bound to my past. I am walking in a new season of financial healing and favor.

Teaching & Testimony

There were patterns in my life I couldn't explain. Every time I'd get ahead, something would pull me back. Money would come then disappear. Unexpected bills, broken cars, family drama, even sabotage from those close to me. It felt spiritual. And it was.

Financial curses aren't just bad habits they're deeply rooted systems passed through generations: poverty mindsets, fear, greed, pride, lack of teaching, and cycles of dysfunction. Many of us were never taught how to manage money because the people before us didn't know either.

But I came to tell you the curse stops here. Jesus paid the price, and you have authority. But you must also act. We break curses with both the sword of the Spirit (the Word) and the wisdom of stewardship.

In my journey, I fasted. I prayed. I repented. I forgave. I tithed in faith even when it didn't make sense. And I watched chains fall off my bank account, my business, my mindset, and my family.

The Breakthrough Strategy

- Identify financial patterns in your family history (lack, loss, bankruptcy, gambling, broken partnerships).

- Renounce those patterns in prayer. Speak aloud: 'I break every generational curse of lack, mismanagement, and sabotage in Jesus' name.

- Forgive the people who mishandled finances in your life. (Even if it's you.)

- Establish new patterns: tithing, budgeting, saving, teaching your children, building.

- Walk in the fruit of the Spirit patience, discipline, peace even with your money.

Faith in Action:

Fast for 24 hours with this focus: 'God, reveal and remove every root of financial bondage.' Then write out a family financial prayer and speak it over your household each day for 7 days straight.

Reflection Questions

What financial habits or beliefs have been passed down in your family?

What cycle have you seen repeat that you are called to break?

What's one spiritual AND one practical step you can take this week to break a financial curse?

Back of Book – Final Sections

Final Words: Walking It Out

If you've made it this far, pause for a moment. You haven't just finished a book you've begun a shift.

Financial freedom is not just about money. It's about discipline, healing, identity, and obedience. When God is involved, nothing is wasted not your pain, not your process, and not even your past.

From the streets to stability. From survival to structure. From fear to faith. This is where you start walking differently.

What's Next: Continuing the Journey

Take what you've learned and begin applying it. Start small. Be consistent. Invite God into every decision.

If you are incarcerated, formerly incarcerated, or supporting someone who is, know that you are not forgotten. There is a future beyond the walls.

Financial freedom is available to anyone willing to learn, grow, and change.

About the Author

Dr. Angie Locus-Kelly is a financial literacy educator, entrepreneur, nonprofit leader, and pastor whose life is a testimony of redemption and transformation.

She has served as a foster parent for over 15 years and ministered for over 20 years inside prisons and juvenile detention centers throughout New York. She is the Senior Pastor of Second Chance Agape Worship Center and founder of Each One Reach One Radical Generation.

From the Streets to Financial Freedom is not just her story — it is her mission.

Faith in Action & Reflection Journal

Walking Out Financial Freedom by Faith

Introduction: This Is Where Faith Meets Action

This journal is not about perfection. It is about honesty, obedience, and growth.

You do not have to know everything or fix everything today. You only need to be willing to invite God into your financial life and take one faithful step at a time.

Faith without action is dead, and action without faith is exhausting. This journal was created so you can do both.

Daily Faith + Finance Affirmations

I am a wise steward of everything God has entrusted to me. I walk in clarity, not confusion, concerning my finances.

I am disciplined, focused, and intentional with my money. I break free from fear, lack, and financial anxiety.

I think like a lender, not a borrower.

I prepare with wisdom and trust God completely. My finances align with my faith.

My past mistakes do not define my future success. I am building something that will outlive me.

I leave a legacy of wisdom, faith, and provision.

Reflection: Which affirmation was hardest for me to say today, and why?

Week 1 – Stewardship & Awareness

Scripture: Luke 16:10

Prayer: Lord, open my eyes. Show me where I have been careless, fearful, or avoidant with money. Faith Action: Look at your finances without judgment this week.

Journal Prompts:

What emotions come up when I look at my finances?

Where have I been avoiding responsibility?

What does faithful stewardship mean to me right now?

Week 2 – Discipline & Obedience

Scripture: Proverbs 21:5

Prayer: God, help me do what I need to do even when I do not feel like it. Faith Action: Choose one disciplined financial habit this week.

Journal Prompts:

Where do I struggle most with discipline?

____

____

____

What excuses do I usually make?

____

____

____

How would my life change if I stayed consistent?

____

____

____

Week 3 – Trust & Preparation

Scripture: Proverbs 21:20

Prayer: Lord, help me prepare without anxiety.

Faith Action: Set aside something this week, no matter how small.

Journal Prompts:

What emergencies have caught me off guard?

____

____

____

How would preparation change my peace?

____

____

____

What does trust look like financially?

____

____

____

Week 4 – Identity & Responsibility

Scripture: Proverbs 22:1

Prayer: God, restore my name and help me walk in integrity.

Faith Action: Address one financial responsibility you have been avoiding.

Journal Prompts:

How do I view myself financially?

____

____

____

What does integrity look like in my money decisions?

____

____

____

What am I committing to change?

____

____

____

Week 5 – Purpose & Provision

Scripture: Deuteronomy 8:18

Prayer: Lord, reveal the gifts You placed inside me.

Faith Action: Write down one gift or skill and how it can serve others.

Journal Prompts:

What talents have I ignored?

____

____

____

How can my gifts bless others?

____

____

____

What small step can I take this month?

____

____

____

Week 6 – Legacy & Vision

Scripture: Proverbs 13:22

Prayer: God, help me think beyond today.

Faith Action: Make one decision with future generations in mind.

Journal Prompts:

What was passed down to me?

____

____

____

What do I want to pass down?

____

____

____

What systems can I begin putting in place?

____

____

____

Closing Reflection

Growth takes time. Give yourself grace, but do not give up.

Final Prayer: God, thank You for walking with me. I commit my finances, my future, and my legacy into Your hands. Lead me as I continue this journey.

Faith + Finance Tools & Worksheets

This companion workbook expands the teachings from *From the Streets to Financial Freedom by Faith* into practical, faith-centered tools you can use daily.

Believers Budget Template

A budget is not restriction it's revelation. Use this tool to steward what God has already placed in your hands. Sections include: Monthly Income, Fixed Expenses, Variable Expenses, Savings, Notes & Prayer.

Monthly Budget Worksheet

Use this worksheet every month to track planned versus actual spending and reflect on your habits.

Debt Snowball Tracker

Debt doesn't just affect your money it affects your peace. Track balances and celebrate progress.

Credit Dispute Letter Template

Your credit reflects your name. This template helps you challenge inaccurate or outdated information.

Credit Report Checklist

Identify errors, duplicates, outdated accounts, and inaccuracies with clarity and confidence.

Emergency Fund Planner

Preparation is not fear it's wisdom. Plan, track, and replenish your emergency savings.

Monthly Savings Tracker

Progress is progress no amount is too small. Track consistency over perfection.

Income Streams Brainstorm Sheet

Provision flows when purpose meets action. Identify gifts, skills, and income opportunities.

Generational Wealth Legacy Map

Legacy doesn't start with money it starts with intention. Map out who and what you are building for.

Family Vision Planner

Create alignment around faith, finances, goals, and values as a household.

Financial Affirmations List

Daily declarations to align your mindset with faith, stewardship, and abundance.

Devotional Reflection Pages

Scripture-based journaling pages to reflect, pray, and apply financial wisdom.

Breaking Financial Curses – Healing the Root

Bonus Expansion: Walking in Financial Freedom by Faith

Introduction: This Didn't Start With You

Some financial struggles don't come from bad decisions they come from patterns. Patterns you watched, survived, and were never taught how to break.

If you don't heal the root, you will keep fighting the fruit. This section is about freedom, not blame.

What a Financial Curse Really Is

A financial curse is a repeated cycle that shows up across generations. Lack, fear, mismanagement, guilt around money, and self-sabotage can all be signs of inherited patterns.

Scripture Foundation

Galatians 3:13 Christ redeemed us from the curse by becoming a curse for us. Freedom is both spiritual and practical.

Identifying the Patterns

Reflection Questions:

What money patterns did I grow up seeing?

____

____

____

What habits repeat in my family?

What usually happens when I receive money?

____

____

____

What emotions surface around money?

____

____

____

Prayer of Acknowledgment

God, I acknowledge the patterns that have existed in my family and my own life. I bring them into the light and ask You to reveal what needs healing and release.

Renunciation: Breaking the Cycle

In the name of Jesus, I renounce every generational pattern of lack, fear, mismanagement, and financial confusion. The cycle stops with me.

Forgiveness: The Key Most People Skip

Unforgiveness keeps cycles alive. This includes forgiving others and yourself.

Prayer: God, I choose to forgive and release every person connected to my financial wounds.

Fasting & Focus (Optional)

You may choose to fast from unnecessary spending, impulse purchases, or complaining about money. Use that time for prayer and reflection.

Establishing New Patterns

Breaking a curse requires replacement. New patterns include budgeting, saving, planning, teaching, and speaking life over your finances.

Declarations of Freedom

- The cycle of lack stops with me.
- I am not bound to my past.
- I steward money with wisdom and peace.
- I build wealth with integrity and purpose.
- I leave a legacy, not a burden.

Closing Prayer

God, thank You for breaking cycles and renewing my mind. I commit to walking, thinking, and building differently. In Jesus' name, amen.

Final Reflection

Freedom is not a moment it is a decision recommitted to daily. You are called to build differently.

www.ingramcontent.com/pod-product-compliance
Lightning Source LLC
Chambersburg PA
CBHW050816160726
48004CB00002B/866